Home Again
Simply Country

by
Judy Condon

Library of Congress Cataloging-in-Publications Data
Home Again - Simply Country by Judy Condon
ISBN 978-0-9772309-7-6

Oceanic Graphic Printing, Inc.
105 Main Street
Hackensack, NJ 07601

Printed in China

Layout and Design by Pat Lucas

About the Author

Judy Condon is a native New Englander, which is evident in her decorating style and the type of antiques she collects and sells. Her real passion is 19thC authentic dry red or blue painted pieces. While Judy's professional career evolved as a teacher, Principal and Superintendent of Schools in Connecticut, Judy's weekends were spent at her antique shop, Marsh Homestead Country Antiques, located in Litchfield, Connecticut.

When her husband, Jeff, was relocated to Virginia, Judy accepted an early retirement from education and concentrated her energy and passion for antiques into a fulltime business. Judy maintains a website, http//www.marshhomesteadantiques.com and has been a Power Seller on eBay® for over eleven years under the name "superct".

With the success of her books and her working relationships with country shops throughout the United States and Canada, Judy has created a successful wholesale business featuring hand-poured primitive wax pieces and other handmade country accessories that she sells wholesale to country shops.

Judy has five children and five grandchildren and lives in Spotsylvania, Virginia with her husband Jeff.

Judy's first seven books in the "simply country" series, *Country on a Shoestring, Of Hearth and Home – Simply Country, A Simpler Time, Country Decorating for All Seasons, As Time Goes By, Country at Heart* and *Welcome Home* have been instant hits. Judy may be reached through her website or her email address, marshhomestead@comcast.net

Introduction

There are so many clichés about 'home'; 'home is where the heart is', 'there's no place like home', and 'home sweet home' to name just a few. We often banter them about lightly.

Although my husband Jeff and I reside in the state of Virginia, we are fortunate to own a home on an island where we hope someday to retire. It is an island which has within the past two years voted for its independence and is in the process of writing its Constitution and faces changes un-paralleled in its history. Over the years, Jeff and I have established long lasting friendships with native families on this remote island and have actually taken under our wing a native child in need of educational support. My husband and I feel a personal commitment to make a difference in the life of this child and are trying to help not only this child but to help others on the island by establishing libraries in the schools.

Through this child, I have become peripherally involved in the school system as it struggles with its evolution under an emerging government and the pains inherent with growth and change. While I am here on the island for the purpose of utilizing my educational background to provide workshops for teachers in the instruction of language arts and classroom management, I am working on this my eighth book.

When I am not "on island", there are few days that I don't think of this island and its people. And each time the wheels of my plane touch down, I feel I am home again. It seemed only fitting that the title of this book be *Home Again – Simply Country*.

Table of Contents

Chapter 1

❧❧❧❧❧

Jack and Betty Rhodus

Jack and Betty Rhodus built their house in southern Ohio in 1995. The plans for their home are adapted from the design of the Massachusetts Richard Doolittle saltbox dating to 1717.

Betty purchased the gourds on the front door at a gourd festival in Alabama.

Crafted by an artisan from Tennessee, the whale watch sign next to Betty and Jack's side entrance hangs over a folk art figure made by Jack.

The keeping room extends across the back of the house. An 18thC pewter cupboard with New Hampshire origin retains the majority of its early paint. Betty has filled the top with her extensive treenware collection which, with the exception of one or two pieces, is all American. The stack of firkins on the side was purchased over twenty years ago on buying trips to New England.

The portrait over the mantel is oil on a wide board and dates to the 1830's. On the mantel, English pewter chargers provide a back-drop for Ohio pewter teapots and a late 18thC ratchet light that is marked and signed Grant County Kentucky.

The Brewster armchair is a reproduction. Over it, a Massachusetts wall box held pipes and in the drawer, tobacco. The early broom is actually a shaved log with a handle. The large hornbeam on the hearth was deaccessioned from a museum in Williamsburg. A New England tap table dating to the 18thC has splay legs, rose head nails and original Spanish Brown paint. The banister back chair in early red paint is from Deerfield, Massachusetts and still has its early seat. Jack and Betty bought the pheasant at an antique show. On the early pegged rack found in Ohio, an 18thC pouch and powder horn are hung.

Sitting on the ledge of the 'cage bar' is an American hand blown chestnut bottle, so named because of its color. It differs from an onion bottle, not only because of its color, but the fact that a chestnut bottle dates to the 18thC and an onion bottle to the 17thC.

The tavern table in front of the window is a Maine tavern table with stretcher base and single breadboard top. A beehive bowl and trencher in green paint from an estate in New York are displayed on the top.

Sitting in the center of the room, an early Pilgrim era William and Mary tavern table has heavy bulbous turnings and a heavy removable scrub top. It is pegged throughout. On the floor next to it is an American 18thC lighting device from New Hampshire.

Betty's kitchen is compact and galley style. Over the stove hangs a huge breadboard lapboard. On the counter, an early tool holder has become a make-do spoon rack.

In the center of the dining room, a circa 1810 hutch table was dry scraped down to reveal the original red paint. Surrounding the table are 18thC banister back chairs, two of which are from Deerfield, Massachusetts. The large beehive bowl is early New England. The 18thC Queen Anne chest holds an early document box, an inkwell and quill, as well as an American pewter candlestick. The woman's clothing in the oil on wide board dates it to circa 1830's. Just barely noticeable are the eyeglasses she wears on the top of her head.

The salmon step back dates to the 1820's and is filled with bail handled pantry boxes, books and diminutive treasures. The child's Windsor chair beside it has splay legs and green over early red paint. It was found in Kentucky. The doll was purchased from the estate of an 80 year old woman. Betty brings her dolls to life by giving them names. This one is named Papa Joe after Betty's grandfather. The doll wears its original clothes and has a hand drawn face.

The sofa with heart back is a reproduction covered with Lindsey-Woolsey. The portrait is of New England origin and dates to the 1830's.

The primitive candle stand is from the Virginia Shenandoah Valley and holds a reproduction iron rush light.

A tom turkey is suspended from the ceiling over the mantel. The oil on board portrait is New England. An early powder horn dated 1711 and signed JP (possibly John Price of New Jersey) rests on the mantel. The iron shoe form belonged to Betty's ninety-nine year old mother. In the center of the mantel is an early wooden match holder (with its original matches) in old Windsor green paint.

On page 13, a stretcher William and Mary tavern table with scrub top sits in front of the camelback sofa in the Rhodus' living room. Both oil on board portraits are signed Belknap.

The whale tail hanging shelf is early and of New Hampshire origin. On the first shelf, an early little chest with attic surface sits next to a horn cup with the name Davis embossed on the front. Davis was Betty's mother's maiden name. There is also a small tape loom behind the candle and an early mirror. Thumb-sized leather books are on the second shelf.

The armchair is from the William and Mary period and has large turnings. The seat is an early replacement. The early pine candle stand is from Kentucky. The stool in front of the banister back chair was carved from a tree. The portrait is early oil on canvas with New England origin. It is in its original frame and signed by the artist Howes. On the back it says "age 19, 1836".

A large apothecary with early red surface is all original and was found in Fall River, Massachusetts. On top is a Mt. Lebanon Shaker seed box acquired the day before I arrived to photograph Jack and Betty's house.

The sampler over the mantel is a genealogy sampler wrought by Eunice Kindle 1832 from Ludlow Massachusetts.

'Katie', named after one of Jack and Betty's granddaughters, is a Greiner-type doll. The doll sits in a chair which belonged to Betty's mother. The chair was given to Betty's mother as a Christmas present when she was seven years old.

The buttr'y at the back of the house is the first room you enter from the side door and it is filled with primitive treasures. The tall cupboard is poplar and is over eight feet tall. Betty's aunt called her one day about thirty years ago from Indiana and said she had found a cupboard in a chicken house she knew Betty would like. Betty rushed right over and bought it and then spent days and gallons of water to remove the chicken residue which covered it. The ladder back with original green surface is early.

To the left of the cupboard, an old dry sink lined in zinc has an old wooden drain board. The mat beneath it is made of cornhusks. The butter scales are early. Hanging on the wall is a wooden stirrer from Pennsylvania.

Early milk crocks line the floor on the other wall. An early spoon holder hangs next to the shelves holding pantry boxes, firkins and smaller crocks. Dried red peppers are suspended from the ceiling. A large hornet's nest, found on the side of the road, is mounted in the corner. An early herb grinder can be seen in the picture below left. The feed sack on the top shelf is from Garrett County in Kentucky, Jack's home.

The cherry pencil post bed is a reproduction. The French toile canopy in black and white is new. The bed table, dating to the 1840's, was made by Spain Hower, an early cabinetmaker from Jack's hometown in Kentucky.

The table at the foot of the bed is a decorated drop leaf dating to the 1840's with New England origin. Early wallpaper boxes are stacked on top. The chest shown bottom left is a Queen Anne chest of drawers in old red paint dated 1786. A reverse painting on glass mirror above it is early.

The Queen Anne chest shown bottom right is New England. The wallpaper box on top is lined with 1830 dated newspaper. The chair beside it is an early loom chair.

The tiger maple post bed is a reproduction and is covered with Lindsey-Woolsey blankets and quilts. The doll on the floor is a new piece. The ragdolls on the bed are early and have great character.

The country Queen Anne chest in red was found in Kentucky. The doll was found in New Hampshire. Two large wallpaper boxes are stacked on top. The bottom box has a scene of a horse and buggy.

The bed above right, is actually an 18thC press bed, located in the room Betty calls the grandchildren's room. The trundle bed below it has wooden green rollers. The early tiger maple bed table holds family portraits and a leather bound book with Betty's grandfather's glasses. The shelf above the bed holds a collection of early stuffed children's toys, all of which show signs of having been loved

Vintage textiles hang next to an early cupboard from Kentucky.

Jack and Betty are proprietors of Plain & Simple Log Cabin Antiques, *located behind their house in the 1836 Archibald Thompson cabin they transported from Kentucky.*

They also participate in Nashville at Music Valley and other local shows.

Jack and Betty may be reached through their website www.plainandsimpleantiques.com, at (513) 932-9282, (513) 607-4996, or email at wb8ewm@go-concepts.com

Chapter 2

Ted and Pat Isue

Ted and Pat Isue, both retired teachers, built their home in North Canton twenty-nine years ago. Ted and Pat have collected for thirty years and prefer primitives. They started off, as many of us did, saving until they were able to buy a quality piece. Although Ted said they rationalized that their purchases were an investment, they were more influenced by wanting to live with a particular piece. One of their friends, Paige, mentioned that Ted and Pat had simplified their home in the past few years. What I observed was a beautifully decorated home with wonderful early antiques and newer country accessories integrated into each room.

The front louvered door is lined with a screen, invisible to the outside but which allows air to flow into the house, while at the same time ensuring privacy.

The tall clock in the front foyer is Scottish circa 1830. The drop leaf table is 19thC with a wonderful red wash. An early-lidded basket sits on top.

In a passageway from the front hall to the back of the house towards the kitchen, an early jelly cupboard with dry blue paint holds a covered treen storage container and early grinder. The tin sconces adorned with bittersweet are new pieces.

Upon entering the living room to the left of the front entrance, the mantel is a focal point in the room. Ted and Pat purchased the portrait at the Western Reserve Antique Show a number of years ago. An early green onion bottle simplifies the mantel. On the hearth are two early doll cradles. One holds a 19thC doll given to Pat and Ted by a friend.

The hanging Connecticut wall shelf, circa 1800's, is a whale tail, so named because of its shape. It holds early boxes, early lighting, a small silhouette and early basket.

A collection of spatter ware is displayed in the large maple two-piece step back cupboard.

The tall corner cupboard is early 1800's and holds some of Pat's large collection of quilts. The chair and candle stand are early 19thC.

Pictured below left, the light on the early Empire desk is one of two identical pieces Ted and Pat own. A vintage globe sits in the middle of two early red ware pieces on top. The watercolor of a father and son to the left is a new piece painted by folk artist Paige Koosed of Ohio.

The dining room to the right of the foyer contains an extensive collection of old and new red ware.

The red ware on the server shown above is primarily antique.

The circa 1832 pine cupboard shown above right is ideal for displaying some of Pat and Ted's spatter ware and granite ware. A sugar cone and nippers rest on the shelf next to a red ware bowl holding apples.

The cupboard right is a reproduction and holds assorted pieces of red ware and early dough bowls on the bottom.

The Isue's kitchen workspace is "u" shaped with an early butcher block in the center serving as an island. The sink is a Kohler farm sink.

A small mustard painted open cupboard is filled with pottery, crocks and containers on the bottom. A graduated set of yellow ware and mold are on the top.

Shown left, the pie safe with original tins and dry blue paint enhances the color of the salt glazed two-gallon cake crock on top.

A friend of Ted and Pat's made the apothecary on the floor from a single piece of an old walnut board. The apothecary above it with porcelain knobs is old.

A tall stepback with blue paint is seen from the kitchen area. Standing next to it, a stack of early painted firkins adds more color to the room.

Suspended from the mantel, an assortment of early tin and iron cooking utensils is displayed. On the hearth sits an early tin roaster.

In front of the sliding glass doors leading to the screened porch at the back of the house, a double-seated buggy bench with original red paint holds a quilted pillow.

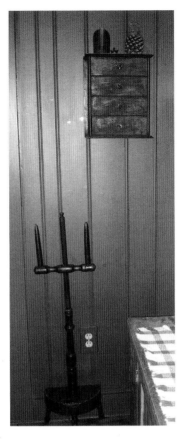

A vintage coffee grinder sits between an early mustard and cinnamon tin on the two-door cupboard in paint abutting the kitchen counter.

Tucked in the corner, a 19thC standing wooden candleholder sits beneath a 19thC small spice box with attic surface.

Pat and Ted use the screened porch at the back of the house as much as they can. The small dry sink and standing cupboard are both pine and early. The drop leaf table and matching chairs were purchased at the Zoar Antique Show.

On the patio, a pond-less waterfall provides tranquility. The base is a deep pit filled with stones so that the water is prohibited from forming a pond. During the winter, Ted removes the pump to prevent freezing.

A late 1700's bowl with wide rim hangs on the side of a dry painted blue jelly cupboard. Pat has wrapped bittersweet around the rim of the bowl adding color and texture to the corner.

The early bucket bench, holds a 19thC blue painted bucket and tin pie keep among other early pieces.

Pat and Ted married the pine hanging cupboard and early scrub top pine table with original red paint on the base.

On the other side of the kitchen, Pat and Ted have used soft cranberry tones and light gold painted trim in the family room.

Shown left, a paint-decorated two-drawer mule chest in black and red is a new piece.

The Isues found the large pine step back in New Philadelphia. The desk beside it is actually a standing dough box which holds early chalkboards. The sampler hanging above the dough box is signed and dated 1845.

The 19thC child's chest in blue paint holds a small box and another of Larry Koosed's animals. The clock above the reproduction bench done by Sally Whims is a family piece and dates to 1875-1880.

Ted and Pat remodeled their downstairs area into a tavern room five years ago. Enhancing the overall look of the room, Ted and Pat hired a mason to lay the floor with half bricks. The oval table shown left was purchased from Marge Stauffer.

Ted and Pat elected to create an open bar space as opposed to a cage bar. A small wall shelf holds pewter cups and charger.

The table below was purchased at the Pine Tree Barn. It is hand planed giving it an early look. The chairs are reproductions.

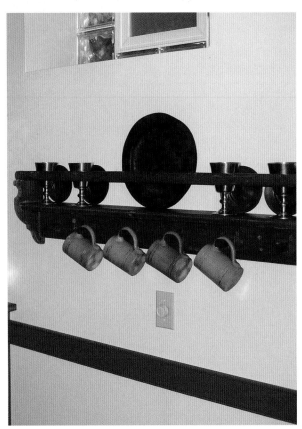

Pat found the Family Heirloom Weavers coverlets and pillow covers at Picket Fence Antiques in Dalton, Ohio. The small watercolor over the bed is a folk art piece done by Paige Koosed. The tiger maple chest was purchased at the Zoar Antique Show.

Below right, the 19thC lift top desk in maple may be Shaker.

Pictured right, the vintage quilt in blue and white matches the trim in the room. The watercolor of two cows above the bed is again a Paige Koosed creation.

The small corner cupboard is a new piece. A hanging cupboard is also a reproduction and holds an early basket and hand-carved folk kangaroo.

The red and black lift top chest is mid 19thC.

Pictured below, Ted and Pat used pine tops on each of their vanities in the up and downstairs bathrooms. Note the interesting faucet replicating an early water pump in the bathroom on the first floor.

Ted and Pat have been "cat sitting" their son's two cats while he has been deployed. They've carried the feline theme in the third guest room with an early paper mache cat on the bed and a folk art painted watercolor above the headboard. Pat has used early red and white quilts as coverlets.

Shown left, a late 19thC tiger maple Empire style chest fits perfectly in the corner of the room.

The vinegar grain painted chest is early 19thC. The unique shaped tin sconce over it is a new piece.

The fourth room upstairs is used as the study or computer room. Pat and Ted purchased the sofa at Picket Fence Antiques. The six-board chest is early. Tucked in the corner, a bucket bench dating to the 1840's holds a few vintage quilts.

Chapter 3

Amy Eschelman

Oftentimes a house will exhibit special characteristics and Amy Eschelman would be the first one to say that her entire house is a "make-do"! Nestled in a quiet residential neighborhood northeast of Columbus, Ohio, Amy's 1868 house, determined by newspapers found under the attic floor boards, was previously owned by an elderly woman from whose estate Amy purchased the house in 2007. After power washing the early original brick and removing layers of pink paint, Amy spent part of last summer landscaping a small country garden in the front of her home and a patio on one side in the back. Stepping through the door, you enter the living room where Amy has created side tables from stacked early boxes, primitive make-do shelves and even cupboards. Amy says she travels within a seven mile radius essentially to find her materials and pieces. She uses old scavenged boards from early abandoned barns and has the good fortune to have a friend with a late 1800's sugar shack where some of her materials have originated.

Amy found the wonderful table with dry red paint in the sugar shack's basement. Amy built the shelves on the side of the fireplace, incorporating an old cabinet in the center. She painted the sign over the mantel. Amy found the bench on the mantel, with permission, in an old abandoned house. It holds three crocks found at yard sales. The old door was found on the side of the road.

Amy liked the early blue paint on the board hanging on the wall. It serves no purpose other than that of appreciation for the wonderful early dry paint. An early bench in chippy white paint below it holds some vintage textiles. Amy reports that her parents have now become involved in her hunt for primitives at an affordable price and often appear at her door with treasures.

In the front corner of the living room, a small round table with two painted chairs found at yard sales, stand beneath a wooden candle holder Amy made.

Amy collects gray granite wares displayed on the shelf in the hallway to the back of the house. The cupboard below has special meaning as it was made with pieces of wood from her former house.

Amy made the fabric primitive platform sheep as well as the small primitive shelf above it.

Amy inherited the cabinets and counters painted bright pink. After painting the cupboards an early red, Amy creatively covered the counter with two boards from the 19thC sugar shack. Adding wooden supports allowed her to stack a smaller tray on top to hold bowls and treen. Early feed sacks hide the bottom storage space under the counters.

To break up the red color, Amy faced the end of an upper cabinet with matching sugar shack wood.

Looking into the kitchen from the hallway, the window fills the room with light. An old branch holds hanging herbs. The lantern hanging in front of the small primitive wall cabinet with attic surface belonged to her Dad and was one he used when coon hunting.

A neighbor planned to dispose of the cupboard right. It had drawers and a glass top but what Amy saw was a cupboard with doors and an open top. Using two doors from an old piece she found in a barn, she removed the glass and painted the whole piece red.

Amy used an old four panel door, which she attached to wooden legs, as a headboard.

Amy's welcoming home exemplifies the definition of a 'home made with love'. A very young single grandmother who enjoys creating in her small workroom at the back of the house, Amy sells her unique pieces at the Simple Goods Show in Ohio in November and annually at the Mt Vernon, Ohio show. She may be reached via email at aeshelman@columbus.rr.com or at (740) 654-1723.

Chapter 4

Andi Teter

Andi Teter bought her 1834 stone house in Medina County, Ohio thirteen years ago and was a collector long before that. Now as a recently retired math teacher, Andi has time to concentrate on antiques and pursue an outlet for her creative talents, which you will see evidenced at the end of the chapter. She particularly likes working with her hands and is in the process of remodeling a basement room into an early tavern.

An enclosed area off the side of the house provides a quiet setting even after the flowers have finished blooming. An old farm wagon with an American flag can be seen from the road.

Andi remodeled the large side porch within the past two years, replacing windows and extending the season for using the room. A small lift top round table sits in front of the newly made couch and holds a canvas duck.

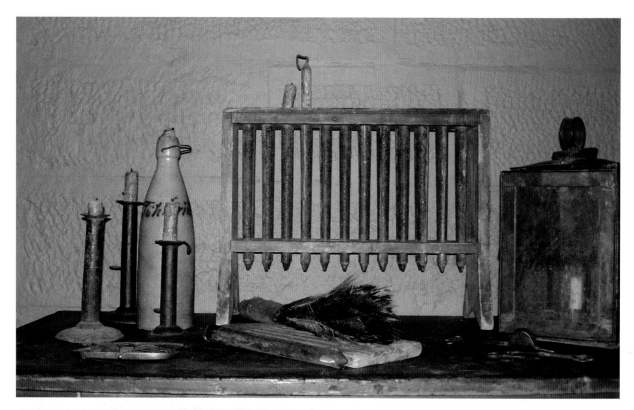

The jelly cupboard in dry red wash has a single paneled chamfered door. On top are a standing candle mold, hogscrapers (above), and an unusual shaped punched tin lantern purchased at Bobby Preiss' Antiques in Westfield, Ohio.

Pictured below, Andi found the early oil portrait on board on eBay®.

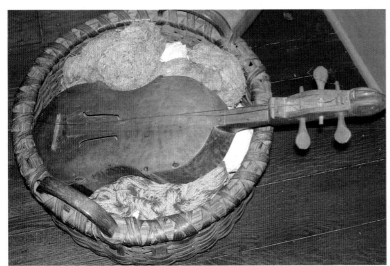

A vintage decoy nests on each windowsill. On the bench, Andi has placed an early dry red painted lift top box. The wooden candleholder seen in the foreground was also purchased at Preiss' Antiques.

Andi feels that the circa 1820's oil portrait, framed in gold leaf over the couch in the livingroom, adds a bit of brightness to the room. The tilt top chair table holds a dough bowl of gourds. Tucked in the corner is an early yarn winder and basket of flax. Andi found the early violin at a flea market for next to nothing, as the holes in the front are not symmetrical. It is handmade and square nailed.

Pictured top left, Andi made the hanging candle dryer, which is suspended in her living room.

Top right, hanging on the door leading from the porch to the living room is a Lindsey-Woolsey man's handmade coat that dates to the 1840's.

The dress hanging on the door is perhaps Amish and dates to the early 1900's. The broom next to it is an early Amish piece. The round table in the center of the room has a stretcher base with old red paint. A large beehive bowl in early paint holds gourds on the table.

A New England jelly cupboard sits under a drying rack filled with herbs. On the top, a carrier is filled with raw flax. A stack of pantry boxes is nestled in the corner.

Andi has hung herbs in the corner with a hanger she made from a dried top of a Christmas tree!

Andi found the red cupboard at the Hartland, Indiana Antique Show. Early red ware and treen are displayed on the shelves. On either side of the unique oval shaped rye basket are two treen sugar bowls. The bowl on the right is black over red paint.

The carrier with delicate heart cutout is Ohio and sits beneath two painted Shaker oval pantry boxes.

Andi used an early red dough box as a bowl container on the top shelf of the early primitive bucket bench. Firkins and measures with paint sit beneath it.

Pictured right, the white painted standing dough box was purchased at Olde Glory in Waynesville. The bowls beneath it hide electrical outlets. The early red basket holds a portable phone.

Andi waited in line at a little shop in Bolivar, Ohio to purchase the large mustard circa 1840's step back cupboard.

The cupboard is filled with horn cups, horn spoons, treen and early red ware. Her red peel hanging next to the cupboard is early. The portrait has Southern origin and dates to the 1820's.

A piggin, old painted barrel and short handled early broom sit on the floor to the side of the cupboard.

Andi totally gutted the kitchen and rebuilt it without any cupboards or cabinets. Using an early red dry sink, Andi used an old pine board to cover the top, which provides a counter top and extends the width of the dry sink.

Andi used a wall oven on the bottom of her stove and covered it with old batten board doors.

An early sage green cupboard holds some old but mainly newer pieces of red ware. One of Andi's favorite pieces is the old sign in chippy white paint which she found at a flea market for about $50. The Jersey Coffee bin was a perfect match for it.

The long handled broom is made from a shaved log. The edges are pulled down and tied together and a handle is added. Andi admits to having a passion for these and has a number of them displayed throughout the house. Andi has a number of cats which she has rescued. Note the use of the early child's potty seat as a holder for the cat's dish. A 19thC bucket bench in red holds two large dough bowls. The bowl on the right is a beehive with an early patch. Two firkins with paint sit on the lower shelf; one of them has buttonhole loops.

Andi has used the back entranceway to display more of her collections. Zinc lidded pantry jars are filled with spices and herbs. An early folk art house sits on a wonderful mustard worktable. Andi's collection of cookie cutters is 'strung' on a vintage corn dryer.

Atop the early cupboard with mustard paint, an 1880's double horse and buggy are shown beside two bail handled pantry boxes with paint.

A small half bath off the back entrance continues the gray and mustard theme with a tall slim chimney cupboard used to store towels.

On the landing in the stairway leading to the second floor, Andi has hung an early fire bucket in dry weathered blue paint from a branch hook. The tall clock is English and dates to circa 1820. Below a shelf of leather bound books, a large horse, perhaps once a child's platform toy, has an early wooden form. The apothecary has original blue paint on the sides and drawers which are all chamfered. The fraktur is Pennsylvania.

Andi painted the blue bed herself to
match the six-board chest at the foot of the
bed. The linens on the bed are all handmade
while the hanging textiles are European
men's nightshirts which Andi buys on eBay®.

Andi elected to unscrew the folk art horse
from the rocker and display it that way on
the floor in the corner.

The wonderful small chest in blue retains its original snipe hinges and dates to the early 19thC. The large white basket serves as a bed for one of the cats.

In the upstairs bathroom, Andi uses a tin candleholder to store her toothbrush and toothpaste. More European shirts hang on the back wall.

Over the tub, an early laundry fork, used to stir and remove clothes from the tub, has chippy white paint.

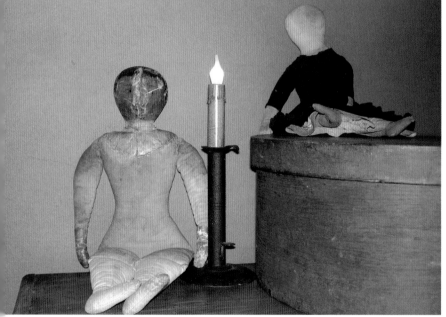

Early textiles hang from a wooden peg rack on the wall in the guest room. The mustard chest, circa 1820, with single wide board fronts holds a few of Andi's early dolls from her collection. The doll on the left has a wooden head and old painted face.

The rocking chair in the corner provides a spot for three more early dolls with old painted faces and original clothing.

At the end of the hallway, two Greiner dolls dating to the mid 19thC sit under a small shelf filled with leather books and a small bear.

The third bedroom serves as Andi's workroom, where she creates very primitive early Santa figures, such as the one featured in the chair and another hanging from the peg rack.

A basement room, which Andi referred to as the cat's room and 'a mess', was beautifully arranged with early painted cupboards and smalls. An early dough box provides a bed for one of the cats.

Andi is in the process of restoring this room (below) and a large room next to it in the basement for incorporation into the living space of her home. The room next to it, which Andi asked me to wait to photograph until it was completed, contains a large beehive fireplace original to the house and all of the early cooking utensils left by the previous owner.

Chapter 5

Lorraine and Jim Kamp

When Lorraine and Jim built their saltbox colonial in 1974 in northern Ohio, it was the first in the area and people thought they were building a barn. They found their plans in a magazine and being in their late 20's and newly married, were on a limited budget. They've lived in the same house and have collected antiques since then. When not paying for kid's braces or college tuitions, Lorraine and Jim invested in antiques. They still have many of their first pieces, but in other cases have "upgraded" their overall collection.

The stretcher base tavern table was purchased from Marge Stauffer and holds a green onion bottle and an early iron candleholder, circa 1750-1820 from a private New England collection. The blackened wax pineapple was made by Marsh Homestead Country Antiques and was a gift from a friend.

At the end of the living room, the late circa 1740's cant back cupboard retains its original rose head nails and cotter pin hinges. It is probably Massachusetts and is one of Lorraine and Jim's favorite pieces. It holds a collection of old pewter and blue Canton china.

The iron diamond shaped sconces over the mantel are early 19thC. The portrait is a copy of an original Lorraine had seen in *Early American Life* magazine in the 1990's. With permission, she commissioned a local artist to copy the original.

The cherry candle stand in front of the hearth dates to around 1820.

The Hepplewhite table and Chippendale chair were purchased from an Ohio dealer in the 1970's. The book on the table is a late 18thC dated dictionary. The silhouette, dating also to the late 18thC, is in its original frame.

The sampler above the table was published in a 1928 book entitled American Samplers. The sampler was done by Lydia Davenport, June 23, 1832. Lorraine couldn't resist purchasing it because it has a blue house at the bottom similar to their home.

The circa 1840's Queen Anne drop leaf table opens to an oval. The chair next to it is a Wallace Nutting comb back Windsor chair.

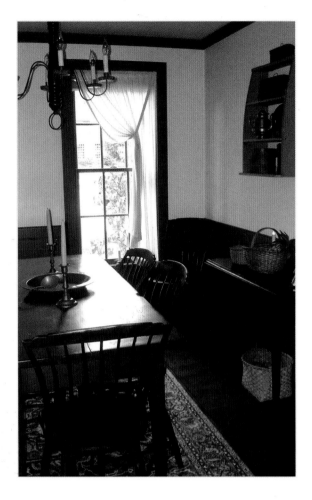

The early 19thC walnut dining room table has a single board top. It is one of the Kamp's earliest purchases. The painted step down Windsor chairs were purchased from an Internet auction.

A small 18thC drop leaf side table along the wall rests beneath a cant back wall cabinet with original salmon paint purchased at the Zoar Antique Show. A tole painted document box and leather books line the shelves.

The small walnut jelly cabinet was another of the Kamp's first acquisitions. The still life above it is mid 19thC.

A small dry sink with tin top holds an early basket. The wall cupboard above it is made of poplar and retains its original red wash.

Lorraine won a large plasma television at a Trade show and had the cabinet to house it built by David T Smith of Ohio.

Collections of pewter plates and porringers decorate the mantel. An early tin box and early iron cooking utensils are hung with heart shaped iron hooks. At the end of the mantel, an early green onion bottle sits next to an early candleholder and pipe box with original black paint purchased at Garth's Auction.

The camel back sofa was purchased from Picket Fence in Dalton, Ohio. Above it, a portrait painted in 1819 by Cooper, is of Stephen Sewall. It was purchased at Marjorie Stauffer Antiques. The chest is late 18thC.

The sawbuck table is 18thC and was purchased in Connecticut. The set of four splat ladder-back chairs are from the Western Reserve Labor Day Antique Show in Hudson, Ohio and were found several years ago. A very lucky find!

The step back cupboard shown right, which holds a collection of red ware, was purchased over thirty years ago. Lorraine said they made payments on it for quite a while but feels it was worth the wait.

Lorraine and Jim remodeled their kitchen in 2005 with the help of a local carpenter and contractor, Dwight Sammet. The farm sink was ordered over the Internet from Designer Plumbing. com. These sinks use authentic London pattern fireclay and have been made for over 100 years by the same Lancashire, England factory.

The red hanging corner cupboard in the laundry room is 19thC Shaker. The antique crock bench is from Picket Fence Antiques.

Lorraine told Jim that if he built her a screened porch off the back of the house, she would find him a glider. Actually she found him two!

An early carrier holds fresh potted herbs on top of a two-door red wash 19thC jelly cupboard.

The blue cupboard in old paint was purchased at a Garth Auction.

Lorraine and Jim found the scrub top pine table at the Zoar Antique Show. The chairs are circa 1820 Windsor birdcage chairs purchased as a complete set.

The small early 19thC red painted cupboard is the perfect size for the top of the stairs hallway. The woman who sold it to Lorraine said she could have sold it a hundred times over before Lorraine had returned to pick it up.

A pristine gold and white quilt is draped over the mid 19thC rope bed in one of the guest rooms. The trim paint is a perfect color and makes a striking statement matched with the dark wood of the pieces. A birdcage armchair, circa 1860 sits next to the oval side table. A six board red chest from the early 1820's has the original till.

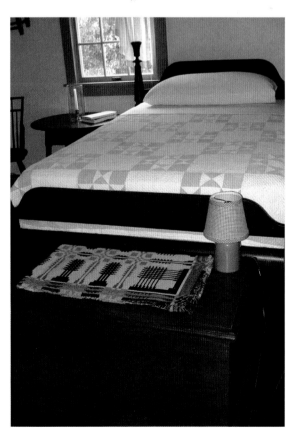

The bed table in the other guest room is from South Carolina. The walnut Chippendale mirror is 18thC and still retains its original glass. The rocking horse is New England, purchased at a shop in Connecticut. It sits on a mule chest purchased at auction. The small wall shelf between the windows holds leather books and a lidded treen storage container.

The upstairs bathroom is painted in New England red. A pine-laminated top covers the vanity. An added shelf over the window provides extended display space for a red ware jug, pitcher, and basket.

The bench at the end of the bed is late 19thC. Lorraine has used gray toned linens as a bedcover and accented it with blue/gray quilted pillows. A small 19thC hollow cut silhouette hangs above the bed.

The chest is 18thC Queen Anne purchased from Marjorie Stauffer. The sampler above it is New England 1793, and wrought by Eleanor Shaw, age 10.

Lorraine constantly upgrades and rents space at Route 43 Antique Mall in North Canton, Ohio. She may be reached through her email at LKamp@neo.rr.com.

Chapter 6

Jack and Judy Weber

Jack and Judy Weber of northern Ohio started to build their home in the late 1990's and finally moved into the house in 2002. They adapted their final house plans from those they found in Country Living magazine. Jack worked for months clearing the land, which was all woods and initially built a barn to house his equipment and serve as a workshop. Jack and Judy took over the house from the builders at the dry wall stage. Jack built all the woodwork, doors, floors and finishing while Judy did all the painting and staining.

In 2008, Jack and Judy built the pavilion, complete with brick floor, in the back where they spend a good part of the summer entertaining. They decorate it appropriately with each season.

Tucked in the corner in the back, Jack and Judy keep a small vegetable and herb garden.

Jack and Judy's dining room table was made by David T Smith of Ohio. Judy had the chairs custom made by Richard Grell from Hudson, Ohio.

Jack and Judy brought the dry painted gray cupboard to an antique show to sell last year and decided if it didn't, they had the spot for it. They're both glad they were unable to sell it. The wonderful 19thC early red box is from the Zoar Antique Show. Judy has filled it with treen and an early winder.

An early bowl is filled with gourds from the garden. Three hogscrapers sit on the table as well; one of them a wedding band candlestick.

Jack and Judy found the green painted cupboard at the Hartland Show in Richmond, Indiana. Judy has used it to display red ware, crocks, baskets and dough bowls. The painted cat on the floor has some age but not an antique whereas the small one on top is early.

The shelf below right hangs in the hallway. Pantry boxes, a Rockingham bowl, baskets and a reproduction child's pull toy fill the shelves. Judy made the sheaf of wheat on the top shelf.

The concealed cabinet to the left of the mantel holds the television and on the bottom, a woodbin with wood for the fireplace.

The wooden lantern on the mantel is made from early wood. The rye basket with wooden bottom is early as is the small chest of drawers at the far right of the mantel.

The sampler is a reproduction patterned after an authentic 19thC piece.

The cabinet over the dry sink was purchased from Primitive Homeplace in Bradford, Tennessee. Judy covered the books with fabric and then coffee-stained them to give them an aged look. An early red ware bowl holds faux fruit. The sheep pull toy is new. The dry sink in early red paint was found in Pennsylvania and required a return trip when it wouldn't fit in the car. Stereo and DVD equipment are stored in it.

A small hanging 19thC pine cupboard was a great purchase at an Ohio auction in Rushville. Jack and Judy have displayed some of their early dry painted decoys.

An open early cupboard in the living room affords Judy wonderful display space for more covered cake crocks, red ware, baskets and even a large carrier which is a newer piece.

An early red ware milk bowl holds gourds on top of the standing dough box in paint. Judy uses it to store flour and sugar. The hanging candleholder above it was purchased at Cows in the Creek. The bowl rack over the counter is early and full of early treen bowls and breadboards. The baskets atop the refrigerator are all early. The cylindrical box is actually a stacking spice box.

Jack bought the old doors and with the aid of an Amish gentleman built the large pantry, shown above. Judy painted the cupboard and uses it to store all her dishware, glasses and pantry items.

The mustard cupboard shown right is a new piece made by a Pennsylvania artisan. On top of the cabinet is an early bucket with wooden staves, early red ware pitcher and zinc lidded pantry jar.

A butt'ry off the kitchen also serves as a laundry room. The boards on the bottom conceal the washer and dryer.

The small mustard box hides the faucets
on the top.

The small wood lidded box with remnants
of red paint is a recent acquisition. The mustard
cupboard over the commode was made by the
same Pennsylvania artisan who made the cabinet
in Judy's kitchen.

The master bedroom is on the first floor. Judy purchased the linen bedcover from Family Heirloom Weavers of Pennsylvania. The 19thC chest in red paint at the foot of the bed was acquired at Nashville. The mule chest in Spanish Brown paint was purchased from Marjorie Stauffer.

Another purchase from Marjorie Stauffer is the mule chest in red, which Jack and Judy use as a bedside table.

The large cupboard in red at the foot of the bed was custom made by Sally Whims. The Windsor chair next to it was one of the first DR Dimes chairs made and is painted black over red.

One of the first pieces Judy ever purchased over forty years ago is the small cherry bucket bench, which she says has had a spot in every room of the house at some point.

Judy found the dry gray painted jelly cupboard in Maine and uses it now to store sweaters. The basket on the top right is an early North American Indian basket with potato stampings on it.

The upstairs landing is almost room size and ample to allow a large wall shelf purchased at Nashville and a scrub surface two-door jelly cupboard.

A navy blue and cream heavy cotton coverlet is topped with a red duvet cover. In the corner of the room, the top of a Windsor birdcage chair is barely visible. Judy found the chest in Ohio, and was one of the first pieces she owned. She prefers to use cupboards or cabinets in place of bureaus or chest of drawers.

More textiles are displayed in the open cupboard found at the Richmond Antique Show. A small black child's rocker holds a child's bear next to it. A child's chest in red fits perfectly in the nook created by the sloping roof. An early red buttocks basket and cricket bench sit on top. The maple rope bed is early.

I couldn't resist stopping to take a picture of the birdhouse in the driveway which I later found out Jack made as a birthday present for Judy.

Although Judy doesn't have a shop, she sells at the Simple Goods Show in Mt. Vernon, Ohio in early November and is constantly upgrading her collection. Judy may be reached at (740) 694-1304.

Chapter 7

Bill Hromy

To say that Bill Hromy has been a collector almost all his life is not an exaggeration. Since a young boy, Bill has been interested in antiques and, more specifically, Shaker pieces. His mother used to take him to antique shops, and when Bill was fourteen, he met Virginia Proust who had an extensive collection. Ms. Proust introduced Bill to Mrs. Kalb of Ohio, whose father had been mayor of Pittsfield, Massachusetts, where Hancock Shaker Village is located. Mrs. Kalb had collected Shaker for years and took Bill around to meet other collectors and to auctions. As a teenager, while working at a gas station, Bill mentioned to his boss and owner that he was interested in buying a Shaker piece but didn't have the money. His boss said, "Now is as good a time as ever to learn about responsibility and how to take out a loan", and he marched Bill over to the bank and co-signed a note with him. While most teenagers were 'throwing money away', Bill worked to save money to buy Shaker pieces. As a result, his collection is extensive. Meeting Bill and photographing his Shaker collection was not only a delightful experience, it was a lesson in

Shaker history. The house, built in 1846 by Barnabas Crane, a sea captain from Bristol, Massachusetts, was previously owned by Mrs. Kalb. The house is surrounded by the Wolf Creek Nature Park which offers Bill a great deal of privacy and solitude.

A large horse-watering trough serves to provide a 'pond' at the edge of the driveway. All of the stones throughout Bill's property were found in Medina County.

A cast stone cat perches in the center of an early cistern cover.

Bill uses the bell on the pole pictured below as his doorbell.

The back entranceway holds a treasure of Shaker history. The stone sink at the back holds buckets and firkins. Beneath it, painted buckets with the Shaker distinctive diamond brackets are stacked and stored.

The small bucket at the corner of the shelf with vertical stripes was made to commemorate a disastrous fire at Mt. Lebanon, New York in 1875. These buckets would have been purchased as gifts in the shop and given to friends. It is made from cedar and sumac which survived the fire and dates to 1880.

The green firkin with pewter top was a field pail used to take water out to the workers in the field.

The bucket shown left in mustard paint is unique because of its size. The diamond bracket is a Shaker 'trademark'.

Shelves or Rockingham, so named because of the actual glaze, fill the buttery. Sponge decorated, they are all Ohio pieces from the Akron area and originally were shipped out on the canal and used for ballast on ships.

In addition to a display of early cutting boards, peels and winnowing boards, Bill has framed hand painted water colored botanicals. Early zinc lidded pantry jars hold spices and herbs. Small tapers are stored in a Shaker box in dry red.

The glass front cupboard in bittersweet paint stores a mixture of transfer ware and spatter ware.

An assortment of early bobbins is held in a primitive wall box.

The drop leaf table in the dining room is birch and typical of Mt Lebanon. The chairs, all with Shaker decals, are called Barlow chairs. Sister Barlow was the last Shaker chair maker at Mt. Lebanon and designed the slightly more Victorian finial used on all her chairs.

The pine cupboard is Ohio and has a canted back. A stack of Shaker seed boxes sits on the top. Shown right, broadsides, used to advertise Maine Sabbath Lake products, are framed and displayed. In the frame at the bottom, an early ribbon, placed on items sold in the gift shop, reads, "I come from home of . . ."

The wall on the left side of the dining room contains a flight of shelves filled with Shaker seed boxes, most from Mt. Lebanon. Graduated stacks of beautiful oval pantry boxes in paint sit on top.

A diminutive Shaker bucket in red hangs above framed labels.

More framed labels hang on the wall above the 19thC bucket bench filled with Shaker oval boxes. The hanging basket is called a feather basket and was used to collect feathers. The lid is attached and won't come off. It slides up the handle and ensures that feathers will remain in the basket and not fly away.

One of Bill's most treasured collections is his assembled set of porcelain from the Mt Lebanon community. The set consists of two patterns that were not from the gift shop but were actually used by the community every day.

Bill calls his living room an 'eclectic mix' but it is all an authentic 'eclectic mix'. An early scrub top pine table with red paint sits in the middle of the room. Four wedding band hogscrapers rest on top. A pair of early-mirrored candle sconces hangs over the mantel and surround a signed and dated 19thC sampler. The short stagecoach rifle was a Kalb family piece left by the Kalbs when Bill bought their house. Beneath Bill's collection of signed and dated 19thC samplers, an 1840's Ohio cherry desk holds treen inkwells, a small mantel clock and leather bound books.

A fire bucket with the initials G.W.C. belonged to George Washington Crane, one of the five children of the house's builder, Barnabas Crane. Bill found it at auction. Below it, sits a #9 Greiner doll with an 1858 label.

The side door with heart cutout was a tradition in early times. The builder of the house would carve a heart in a doorway for his new bride.

Hanging over the 19thC rope bed in Bill's guest room, an early small Shaker loom still has the woven thread intact. Framed beneath it is a pair of Shaker gloves knitted for the Sister's Sabbath day. The gloves have initials of the owner.

Bill borrowed money from his parents to purchase the large Shaker cupboard in mustard paint shown left. A marked Shaker rocker sits on one side and a "swivel" chair, called a revolver, on the other. The Shakers are credited with the invention of the "revolver". An article appearing years ago in Harper's Magazine mentioned that the Shakers invented the 'revolver' which caused quite a stir in the communities!

Pictured above is a model doll which would have been sold in the gift shop.

The dolls shown below are called 'pen wipe dolls' and made to resemble the Sisters in their pleated dresses. These dolls were used to blot the excess ink when writing.

In the glass case, Bill has displayed a collection of Shaker bonnets which would have been sold in the gift shops. The shiny bonnets are made of woven straw and most likely are of Mt Lebanon origin. The duller bonnets are made of poplar, a material readily available to the Eastern communities.

A showcase of early Shaker boxes of varying sizes and materials hangs on one wall in the guest room. Many are lined with silk while others are lined with velvet. The boxes sold in the gift shops were made for a number of uses. The shapes dictated their use. Some held men's shirt collars, ladies sewing items, gloves, or calling cards. The large square ones were handkerchief boxes.

Pincushions and spool holders line the middle shelf.

The Shaker desk in the guest room alcove holds a small stack of oval Shaker pantry boxes. On the floor next to it sits a Shaker hat form and bonnet. Other textiles hang from an early rack.

The Shaker cloak shown below would have been worn to the Meeting House on the Sabbath. The fabric is made using zinc, which not only gives it its shine, but also its ability to resist wrinkles. The Shakers are credited with inventing permanent press fabric. A shelf of Shaker seed boxes stands next to the cloak. The Mt Lebanon community was responsible for most of the sale of seeds and was the first community to actually package seeds in packets.

The cloaks shown above were everyday cloaks and sold to the public. The Shakers imported fabric of high quality and when the fabric was no longer available, they stopped making cloaks all together. These are labeled Heart N Shepherd from the Canterbury Shaker community in New Hampshire.

The chest shown left is a seed chest from Mt Lebanon. Each drawer is sectioned to hold different seeds. A collection of Shaker pincushions is housed in the glass case on the top.

A cabinet full of Shaker medicine bottles, many still holding pills and liquid, have been collected over the years. A Shaker wooden bottle filler sits on the top of the cabinet next to a mortar and pestle.

The Shakers sold dolls in their gift shops, which they imported from Germany, with porcelain or bisque heads. They used many of the fabric scraps from the 1860's to dress the dolls so it is not difficult to determine from which community the dolls originated. This particular doll features a hood lined with iridescent fabric.

A wooden pegged rack suspended from the ceiling in the master bedroom came from the attic of a Shaker dwelling in Hancock, Massachusetts. This would have been used to hold seasonal clothing, which could be hung from either a peg or from the small iron rings using a wooden coat hanger. Most clothing was stored in built-in chests.

A case of fancy brushes with velvet trim and silk ribbons is shown below One of the Shaker industries was brush manufacturing, whereby the brothers turned the handles and the sisters did the finishing. These brushes had many uses but were primarily used to brush men's hats and lady's clothing.

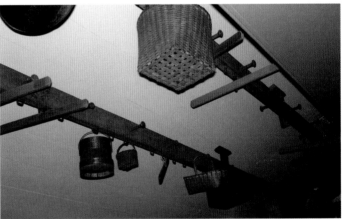

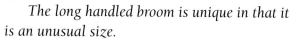

The long handled broom is unique in that it is an unusual size.

Sister Cora Helene Sarle lived at the Canterbury Community from a young age. She was an invalid, and the community essentially left her alone to her painting to keep herself busy. She lived well into her eighties and her paintings are sought-after pieces of Shaker art. Shown left is one of her larger paintings of the Meeting House at the Canterbury community.

Sister Sarle enjoyed painting the landscapes of New Hampshire and often painted them as the seasons changed.

Shown right in the glass enclosure, Bill's collection of Sister Sarle's paintings on tin typewriter containers and pillboxes is extensive and colorful.

Bill's shop, Hromy Antiques in Medina County, Ohio is open Saturday and Sunday from 10:30am to 5:00pm or by chance or appointment. Bill may be reached at (330) 239-1409.

Chapter 8

Joe and Mary Flegle

Joe and Mary Flegle of Canal Winchester, Ohio have been collecting antiques for over sixty years. Originally from Pennsylvania, they moved to Ohio when Joe, who worked for the electric company, was transferred to Columbus. Mary worked part time in a shop in Ohio, giving her first chance at some wonderful pieces.

Their home, located in the historic district, was built in 1790. Mary and Joe had the log house, which dates to 1770, moved to their property.

Mary enjoys gardening, although she claims not to work very hard at it and just lets it happen. The raised beds and paths stretch across the entranceway to the house at the back

The highboy shown in the back corner is a reproduction. As Mary says, 'an authentic one might cost $35,000-$50,000'. A small splay leg table in red paint holds a stack of books and an early rush light. The tavern table in red is very early and dates to circa 1810. On top, an apple box with canted sides holds pinecones and small pumpkins.

The hutch table in red is New England. The bottom lifts for storage. The painting above it is a reproduction. A stack of pantry boxes sits on one side of the table while an early 1800's wooden candle stand with turn top sits on the other.

A 19thC New England red painted mule chest holds an early box in paint. The Chippendale mirror above it is a reproduction.

Joe and Mary's dining room table has a two-board top and drawers. The top comes off and was most likely used as a kitchen table for rolling dough. Dating to 1710-1750, it has a stretcher base and remnants of red paint.

The early beehive bowl with red paint holds a dried pineapple. An early small rug is draped on the table.

The early 18thC pewter cupboard in paint is one of Mary and Joe's favorite pieces. The dry paint is exceptional; note the early iron hinges.

Mary's kitchen is a galley style. Within the
past few years, Joe decided it was too narrow
as it was difficult to open the side door without
bumping into the countertop. He pushed out
the wall and added three feet to the room.

Joe made the stone sink in the butt'ry off
the kitchen. The apothecary beneath it is early.
An early piggin sits at the end of the sink and
a collection of early wooden cutting boards
lines the walls.

Mary loves the fireplace in the keeping room and says they spend most of their time there. The wreath above the fireplace is dried and hangs between early cooking utensils. Look at the delightful cutouts of the skewer-holder. The round table in red has a stretcher base and is early. Mary likes the shelf underneath it for displaying an early bowl. The red ladder back beside the hearth is 18thC and stands next to a large piggin in red paint.

The large early step back cupboard fills one wall between the windows and holds an array of beautiful early painted pantry boxes.

Joe and Mary use the finished room in the basement for entertaining and said they often have large holiday parties. The black stretcher-base table is early and has a two-board scrub top.

An early bucket bench in paint holds a crock filled with drieds. Under it is a small stack of pantry boxes and an early red bucket. The ladder-back chair is early.

The broom next to the vanity is early and could perhaps be Amish.

Mary's Dad made the entire village beneath the tree which Mary leaves up all year. She remembers her Dad making it in the 1920's and is one of the fondest memories she has as a child. Being from Pennsylvania, the village is designed with a fort reportedly to be Fort Legonier. The village is so extensive that Mary is able to display only half of what her Dad built.

At the top of the stairs, a large landing resembles another room. Early rug beaters hang on the wall. The red candle stand is early. The Windsor chair is a new piece. The bench is an old church pew.

The Windsor chair shown right is early. Next to it stands an early 19thC wooden candleholder. A vintage douter, used to extinguish the flame, sits on the middle post.

The mother and baby dolls on the 19thC rope bed are reproduction Shaker pieces. Two stacked cupboards in red hold baskets. The doll chair on the floor next to the cupboard is early, as is the bear.

Mary decided to place the large four-poster bed in the center of the room, and it looks as though that's just where it should be. The crewel pillows provide contrast to the woven linen coverlet and pick up the blues in the cloth. A small table and lift top desk are tucked in the corner.

The highboy is a new piece and holds a large lidded basket, perhaps North American Indian. An Amish bonnet sits on top of a pantry box stack on the floor beneath it.

Two early 19thC blanket chests with blue paint are stacked at the foot of the bed.

Joe says this is his favorite room! And it is gorgeous. Overlooking a well-kept lawn, where Joe says they have had many outdoor parties, the patio captured the last bits of sunlight.

Although Mary is not doing as many shows as she once did, she does a show in Lancaster, Ohio. She has decided that even at 80 years old she is going to re-open her antique shop on the property. By the time this book is published, the shop, Mary Flegle Antiques, should be in full swing. Mary can be reached at (614) 837-2217.

Chapter 9

❧ ◆ ☙

David and Jody White

When David and Jody White first returned home to their native New England from Florida, they rented a house in Maine while they looked for a piece of land on which to build. David found a perfect eighteen acres but unfortunately it had a house and barn on it and was too close to the road. He called his wife Jody and said, "We've got to buy this property". Jody wasn't interested because of the proximity to the road but when David said he would move both buildings back from the road, Jody said, "You're nuts", and agreed. Located in

Kennebunk, Maine, Fairview Farm has a magnificent westerly view of the sunsets. The house, built in 1803, was ready for occupancy on David and Jody's wedding anniversary, June 14, 1994.

David and Jody spent considerable time visiting David's parents in England, which explains in part that Jody's gardens are patterned after an English knot garden. They purchased granite from an old house two hours away and spent three summers with three tractors building granite walls and walks, while at the same time creating proper drainage so the Maine winters would not cause frost heaves. Jody likes an orderly garden so that all the plants are visible while using millstone and statues for interest.

The kitchen was completely remodeled two years ago. David and Jody used mottled purple slate from a quarry in Poultney, Vermont. A center island holds cook books and provides a large surface for working.

David and Jody had just begun to remodel their living room when I was there. The clock on the mantel is a New Haven steeple clock. The painting above the mantel is a reproduction of the famous painting of the girl in red dress.

A 19thC round table with stretcher base holds fresh cut flowers from the garden.

Two 19thC samplers hang on the wall opposite the door. They are both signed and dated by the Read sisters who wrought them.

David essentially took the front door apart and rebuilt it. The transom is original to the house. The hardware was found in Maine.

The tall clock is English. While visiting David's parents in England, one morning David went to the butcher shop and stopped at an antique store where he found the clock. David borrowed money from his parents who ended up holding the clock for David. When his parents moved back to the United States, they presented the clock to David and Jody as a gift.

Jody is descended from Sir William Wallace and on the mantel is a statue of him. Pieces of Staffordshire and a Welch pitcher are also displayed

A magnificent 19thC barrel back corner cupboard with blue paint holds more of Jody's porcelain. The secretary shown below right is cherry, a New England piece dating to the late 18thC. David and Jody bought it from a picker who found it at a yard sale! Above the desk are William Bartlett prints of black and white etchings, which Jody and David had colorized. They depict a variety of scenes of the White Mountains in New Hampshire.

David and Jody inherited the English oak corner cupboard.

The tiger maple dining room table is a new piece, as are the chairs.

The oil painting over the mantel in the dining room is signed "A Thomas", and indicates on the back 'Stonebridge near Oxford'. The mantel is lined with pink Lustre ware.

The sideboard is Asian. Above it, a whale tail wall shelf in cherry holds Staffordshire and new and old mocha ware. David made the shelf patterned after a piece he had seen in England.

David and Jody added the transom window over their bed to provide light, but at the same time give them privacy. The chest at the foot of the bed is a Maine piece with grain painting.

The baskets on top are early.

The table shown above is an English card table with a gate leg.

The 19thC tiger maple chest shown above was purchased at the Zoar Antique Show in Ohio.

The small clock, right, stands only three feet tall and was made by the Jerome Company of New Haven, Connecticut. It was designed to compete with the English clockmakers and purposely made smaller to take up less space.

Chapter 10

❧❧❧❧❧

Mary Booth

Mary Booth moved to her 1960's ranch in the small town of Fredericktown, Ohio seven years ago and has transformed her fairly new house into a charming 19thC single floor home. With the help of a friend who totally dug up the front lawn, removed the grass, brought in top soil and built a fence, Mary has created a wonderful country garden right in the middle of a rather urban neighborhood. The bee house is the focal point in the garden. Using rocks, stone wheels and troughs, Mary's garden has tranquility about it.

Mary has used an old water pump with blue paint to create a vignette at the edge of her walk. An old stone trough is filled with small pumpkins. Indian corn dresses up the pump.

Mary and her late husband bought the cherry cupboard shown below at auction many years ago. It was painted white at the time and they put it in the shop but it remained unsold. One day, Mary's husband brought it inside and began to scrape down the white paint to find a gorgeous original blue over red 19thC paint beneath. As Mary says, "then everyone wanted it". Her husband just said, "It's not for sale. It's a keeper"!

The doll hanging on the door was made by Dru Ann McCarthy of Cinnamon Creek in Kentucky. The cupboard holds an assortment of early baskets and one in particular, shown on the top shelf, is a diminutive basket with potato stamping, which Mary bought at an estate sale in Pennsylvania many years ago.

Nestled in a corner is an early worktable in dry red paint. The tin lamp on top is a newly crafted piece. The small cupboard over it holds some of Mary's late husband's butter presses.

The sawbuck table in the center of the room is early and has original attic surface.

Mary found the early hooked welcome rug years ago. A square nailed crusty white paint carrier sits at one end of the mantel. Two bail handled pantry boxes sit at the other end. The large barrel on the hearth is held together with wooden staves and doesn't have one nail in it. Mary's late husband came up with the best idea which she has used for years. To keep the staves tight, Mary keeps a wet sponge inside the barrel. Whenever it dries, she soaks it again. When I think of all the barrels I've thrown out because they dried up and fell apart.

The settle in red is a Sally Whims piece. Mary has many of Sally Whims creations throughout her home integrated with her antiques.

Mary's early painted pieces with muted tones give her entire living room an open and elegant look. The dry sink at the back wall has grungy yellow paint and matches perfectly the tones of the bucket on the top and the large beehive bowl hanging above it. A stack of footstools, all with early paint sits beside it. The gray chest in the foreground is an early mule chest.

In the corner of the room, another small cabinet in "junky yellow", as Mary calls it, holds an early square nailed game board with early red and black paint.

The small box shown right, is a fantastic reproduction made by Matthew Jacks of Pennsylvania. The back is entirely open and its purpose is to conceal a light switch on the wall.

On page 136, the table in the dining room is a Sally Whims piece. Mary uses the early trencher in the center of the table to hold more butter prints. The chairs are newly made by River Bend.

The early Spanish brown painted cupboard in the corner holds an apple box with canted sides.

Pictured right, the red hanging corner is early and was purchased at Garth's Auction. Below it, one of Sally Whims' dry sinks in red holds an early basket. An old blue painted butter churn is placed beside it. Some of Mary's vintage tin cookie cutters are displayed on a primitive make-do shelf.

Below left, a collection of salt glazed crocks fill the early bucket bench with attic surface. Above it, a Sally Whims bowl rack holds early bowls in paint.

Below right, Mary found the corner cupboard in Pennsylvania and didn't care that the door was missing. A hand painted sign on the top reads Homespun Gatherings, the name of her business.

Mary has used an early faded American flag fabric as her curtain. A winnowing board hides her sink. A painted carrier holds early boards.

Mary found the interesting three-door cupboard at a farm auction. It actually has only two sides but Mary found the perfect spot for it. The early dough box, complete with a mouse hole, holds an assortment of dough bowls and cutting boards, one of which has remnants of red paint. An early primitive ladder in the corner holds an American flag remnant.

Some of Mary's white banded and seaweed pattern yellow ware is on display in the early cupboard with salmon paint and tin repair on the door. The boxes on top are wooden advertising boxes. A friend hand painted the Green Beans sign under the painted shelf.

An early dry gray painted dry sink has a small drawer on the side. An old red painted bucket holds potatoes. The hanging green cupboard above the dry sink is early, although the crocks on the top are newer pieces from a Pennsylvania pottery. The tin sconce on the cupboard door is early.

Pictured below right, the early mustard cupboard is grain painted. It holds two newly handmade dolls dressed in vintage homespun.

By the time I called Mary after my visit, the cupboard pictured left, which Mary purchased at Garth's Auction, was loaded in the van ready to be put up for sale at a show.

Pictured on page 141, Mary has managed to find a vintage quilt with blues and tans to match the Sally Whims blue bed. The bed below it is a hired man's bed. The large cupboard in the corner has chippy early ivory old paint.

Perched on a Whim's small wall cabinet, the folk art tin bird was one of Mary's husband's favorite finds.

At the end of the hall, Mary has filled the Pennsylvania 19thC cupboard with early textiles and feather pillows. The rocking horse on top was in pieces in a box when Mary found it at an auction. Her husband rebuilt it.

The early six-board chest is Ohio. The document box on top retains much of its original early wallpaper.

The tool over the bed is a Shaker, all wood, feather bed smoother. Pictured on page 143, the red chest in the corner next to the bed, is a Sally Whims piece.

Mary has been a collector for over twenty-five years and continues to do shows and sell pieces from her home. Mary does the Simple Goods show in November in Mt. Vernon, Ohio and the Back Creek Cabin Show in Jonesboro, Indiana in June. Mary can be reached at (740) 485-0779.

You, my readers, have asked that I include pictures of both the outside and the inside of the homes I feature in my books. In **Welcome Home – Simply Country**, I introduced a new format which I call "house tours" and it has been well received. My plan is to continue devoting a full chapter to each home in future books.

Recently I came across this definition of home: "Home is a place you grow up wanting to leave and grow old wanting to get back to." Judging by the beautiful homes I visit and the devotion we give to decorating our home, Home truly is 'where our heart is' and there truly is 'no place like home'.